Fall of the Rebel Angels

ANDY BROWN is Director of the Centre for Creative Writing at the University of Exeter, where he lectures in creative writing and literature and directs the undergraduate, postgraduate and public creative writing programmes. Originally, he studied Ecology, a discipline that informs both his poetry and his criticism. He was previously a Centre Director for the Arvon Foundation's creative writing courses at Totleigh Barton in Devon and has been a recording musician. He lives in Exeter with his wife and two children.

Books by Andy Brown

Poetry Books
> *Hunting the Kinnayas* (Stride, 2004)
> *From a Cliff* (Arc, 2002)
> *of Science* (Worple, 2001, with David Morley)
> *The Wanderer's Prayer* (Arc, 1999)
> *West of Yesterday* (Stride, 1998)

Poetry Chapbooks
> *The Trust Territory* (Heaventree, 2005)
> *Vital Movement: Reality Street 4-packs No. 4* (Reality Street, 1999, contributor)
> *The Sleep Switch* (Odyssey, 1996)
> *Ode to a BiC Biro after Wittgenstein* (Trombone Press, 1995)

Editor
> *The Allotment: new lyric poets* (Stride, 2006)
> *Binary Myths 1 & 2: correspondences with poets and poet-editors* (Stride, 2004)

Fall of the Rebel Angels

POEMS 1996–2006

ANDY BROWN

CAMBRIDGE

PUBLISHED BY SALT PUBLISHING
PO Box 937, Great Wilbraham, Cambridge PDO CB1 5JX United Kingdom

© Andy Brown, 2006

The right of Andy Brown to be identified as the
author of this work has been asserted by him in accordance
with Section 77 of the Copyright, Designs and Patents Act 1988.

First published 2006

Printed and bound in the United Kingdom by Lightning Source

Typeset in Swift 9.5/13

ISBN-13 978 1 84471 280 9 paperback
ISBN-10 1 84471 280 X paperback

TB

1 3 5 7 9 8 6 4 2

for my wife, Amy,
invisible in every word

Contents

Acknowledgements

These *Poems 1996–2006* are those alone that I wish to preserve in print from the first ten years of my book publication. Many appear as they were first published in individual volumes, others have been edited over the years and it is these final versions I wish to preserve. The writing is organized broadly into four musical movements and appears in no particular chronological order.

Special thanks to those who have generously published and supported my work during this period, in particular: Tilla Brading and Derrick Woolf, John Burnside, Peter and Amanda Carpenter, Ken Edwards, John Kinsella, Rupert Loydell, David Morley, Tony Ward, Anthony Wilson, the team at *Heaventree Publications* and all the editors of the magazines, journals and anthologies where my poems have been published in the UK and abroad. Thanks also to these and other readers for invaluable advice on shaping this and other manuscripts. Acknowledgements are due to the Arvon Foundation and to the School of English, University of Exeter, for providing the time and context within which to write these and other works.

Acknowledgements are also due to the editors of the following publications where some of the latest pieces have been published:

'Littoral' in *Bonfire: an international conflagration*; 'Winter Into Spring' in the *Near East Review*; 'Autumn, Mount Fuji' and 'An Ill Wind' in *Sentence: a journal of prose poetics*; 'The River and the Cathedral', 'Crossing the Sound' and 'Fall of the Rebel Angels' in *Stride Magazine*.

Cover Painting: *The Fall of the Rebel Angels*
by Peter Breughel the Elder, 16th Century

'What I aim to do is not so much learn the names of the shreds of creation that flourish in this valley, but to keep myself open to their meanings, which is to try to impress myself at all times with the fullest possible force of their very reality. I want to have things, as multiply and intricately as possible, present and visible in my mind.'

—ANNIE DILLARD, from *Pilgrim at Tinker Creek*

I

'The self is curved like space.'

—CAROL SHIELDS, *The Stone Diaries*

The Thread

Long before we see the swallows find their way back home
we sense their coming in our blood,
something unnameable, like the sound of the breathing
we come to recognise as our own,
or the strange shrieks of foxes on lake margins,
which remind us that it is, perhaps,
intangible geometries that tie all this together,
or how, sometimes at night, we think we hear
timber falling in a forest we cannot name,
a wooded col on the peak of our loves
and find ourselves blessed by the presence of birds,
trees—a calligraphy of light high in their branches—
and there, in a crack, we find the threads that link us:
the knowledge that all we have to do is change.

The River and the Cathedral

It's certainly a melancholy life;
no joy without an equal ounce of grief,
for what flows through us is ours only
      momentarily—
a reflection caught in an endless plane
of mirrors—like light on a frozen leat,
making it appear our journey's aim
might be the great bend in the oxbow's heart
where sunlight nibbles at the lingering ice
in the overhang—that irresistible tug of how
young rivers *used* to run, fast & bright—
as we welcome the passing of winter,
like toads caught on an iced-up pond.

And yet it also seems that, up ahead,
it might be the city that calls; the city
full of people who would rather be
elsewhere.
      Didn't we notice it,
the horizontal text of the river?   Sure,
we had seen a misted scene take shape,
but that was all compounded of frustration
& desire, wasn't it; our need to run ahead
in spirals, up the steps and banging at the door,
in search of sanctuary; a simple peace?

City Bus Ride

'I have need to busy my heart with quietude.'
—RUPERT BROOKE, 'The Busy Heart'

It is morning in the city. I have boarded a bus,
not knowing where the driver's to, or the route
she will take. Whenever I am able to escape
myself, I ride for hours like this on roads
around the city's parks, with their tall trees
filtering sunlight and their inviting rugs of grass.
When the bus leaves, she goes from a coffee house
where men smoke, drink strong coffee and play
dominoes, even at this hour. The city is vibrant
with motion's music. Desires head in all directions.
Ribbons of roads fan out from the heart and make
the city throb with rhythms of legend & myth—
there is something ancient in her, like the presence
of the Ziggurat of Ur.
                              At the end of a bridge,
where the buildings stand in disrepair, the ritual
of two people shaking hands, cryptically symbolic.
A third man on his knees holds congregation
with a flock of birds. Children hurry past him
on their way to school, bubbling into the distance
like beads of faience in an ancient trader's hands.
'Buzzing with Life,' the girl beside me says, although
it's never Life itself we see; it is the woman
and woman alone we see moving as she walks
between high terraces banked with plants; the flex
in her arms & legs; the torsion in her back.
The world is real in face of our experience
and nothing more. All philosophy teaches that.

Crossing the Sound

Memory is a strange and graceful town:
a comic-opera capital at times,
and other times a busy working port
as migrant terns & plovers see it—
ordered its dry docks; wild its beaches . . .

but on beaches, the idea of *Yesterday*
never happened: twice daily the tides
renew the pristine banks of sand,
pulled by the carapace full moon.
The horizon hovers like a possibility:
how to get there, we think; *to see ourselves
safe against the tide*, asking questions
of the pleated wilderness of sea.

The sea says a change is in order,
the marker buoys clanking bells
softly;   yet we remain rooted,
startled by our own footprints
where before there were none.
Ahead, a sliver of light rises
from the lip of darkness, making us
relinquish all we can't retain; retain
the kick we find in remembering
our island's moods & rhythms
before they vanish in a flicker of wind.

Stes-Maries-de-la-Mer

'*Les Chevaliers?*' you said and we made it in time
to see five riders pass on horseback—those
fabled, snow-white creatures that metamorphose
as they grow, born brown, or black and blanched pure white
by four years old—crossing the quiet inlet of the delta,
serene in the shadow of Juniper trees. Later,
in the cool church, we touched the disused props
of the lame who came to walk; the patches
of the blind who came to see in this haven
of miracles & changes, where the bones of Saints
are carried through the streets each May,
down to the sea in a healing cavalcade.

And later still we also rode those changelings,
our stallions standing firm at first, though throwing
back their heads—the air resonant with insects—
and then, sensing something inexperienced
in the way we held the reigns, bolting through
the shallow lagoons in an explosion of hooves,
our muscles and theirs screaming with the violent flash
of summer, until they dropped us, their muzzles
foaming in sweat and we slumped from our saddles,
shocked and fighting for breath in the chafing grass.

The Water Cycle

(for Sally Meyer)

Framed by fences and telegraph lines
as in Spencer's *Resurrection,*
the mourners trudge uphill until
a Church of Scotland road sign jerks them
left beneath the 'Yes Yes' on the gas tank.[1]
The coffin's borne by hand into the open autumn air,
upon a stripped pine door with stretcher handles.
Stooped & beret'd men march on ahead,
the women drag their '30s shoes behind.
Gulls trace mental lines above the lichen-covered roofs.
Seafood enters port in freezer skips—these graveyards
always sited where the sea and shoreline fuse.
A skein of cloud the length of the horizon
divides the sky & sea, each mirroring the other,
what the other *would be.* The estuary broadens,
the current slows, as life on shore resumes
its common pace. This is all there is then—
one brief crawl up the world's edge; a glimpse of
impossible light. *Outside the wind blew . . .*

---

[1] 'Yes Yes'—a funeral in Tarbert Docks, Isle of Harris, on the day of the referendum for a devolved Scottish Assembly.

From A Cliff

(for George Szirtes)

Say we find ourselves sitting with our feet
over the edge of a cliff, the horizon bending
not only ahead but all around and even inwards,
pregnant in its curvature—this grassy ledge
we call a home, the illusion of an island—
what of the idea we are then; the image conveyed?
Here are our opening arms, high above the truth of it.

As pigeons in a city park begin the day
and test the sky, subsiding into flurried clusters,
we sit as we are, not doing what we are
supposed to be doing, lifeless in suspension;
and what of keeping a notebook of the days
we've made up in our mind? Is that all
this is all about; recorded time?

'An idea is nothing but the start of tears;
the flutter of fear beneath the skin,'
our fingers whisper and that rings true,
not only because ideas become confused,
but also because of speech itself becoming
a part of the pain—speaking of jumping
to swim in the ache of the opening air.

Today spills southward using light as a lure,
drifting into air's anticipation. Inside
its gates, again, voices—the living words
our hearts pick up, all dying of darkness.
We sit abutting change and, yes, it's true, almost
to the point of smiling: we learn loneliness,
with solely a monopoly of spirit to reassure its limits.

Littoral

The ocean wants for nothing but to be
left alone—a dozen tones of turquoise,
mist & spectra. Wrinkled like soft polyps
in their neon castles of coral, your fingers
trace the beach's groynes filigreed by salt
and, as you may now also be thinking it,

the ancients too observed it:
the sustenance of their mother sea; knew how to be
at home with her, from the reef to the salt
marsh, throughout each moment of turquoise,
nudged toward shore by her fingers
like a deepwater swell fanning polyps.

But I have been distracted by the polyps.
The water has shaped me to its
own devices, with persuasive fingers;
it will not let me be
alone with you at the edge of turquoise
and the line of stone breakwaters baked in salt.

We stand now like pillars of salt;
vulnerable as starfish and polyps
washed ashore in storms. This turquoise—
if only we could look into its everyday light; its
marvelous animal; its ships and debris, and be
happy with the chances between our fingers,

like the fisherman who wrapped his fingers
around a bottle, removed the cap, releasing salt
and a cloud of smoke, finding himself to be
in command of a djinn, blooming like a polyp
filled with fearful magic from deep within it;
a terrible shade of turquoise.

Sometimes when I think about the turquoise
depths of the bay; its intractable granite fingers;
the sea seems almost to be
too restless to ever return to; too salty
to anymore sustain us; anemones; polyps.
But like a pair of dolphins breaching through it

I know we must be returned to its saltiness.
Above us and beneath us—turquoise; our fingers, flippers;
our eyes like polyps, glowing with the wonder of it.

Vertigo

(i.m J.H.)

The curved horizon stares so silently,
inviting you to your ancestral shore—
a ship set loose on seas of memory.

A bird beginning flight, you pick up speed.
Above, the terns that saw young Icarus fall.
The curved horizon stares so silently.

A voice within the rock demands you leap.
Suddenly you're heavenrushing; through the door—
a ship set loose on seas of memory.

The names of those who leave us rest in peace,
as dust settles on the catafalque.
The curved horizon stares so silently.

Disappearance holds a thread of mystery.
You jump the nest and fly, begin to fall—
a ship set loose on seas of memory.

I look down at the slip face and the roiling sea.
As if arranged, the breakers part and roar.
The curved horizon stares so silently
at ships set loose on seas of memory.

Some Kind of Sea Light

'The root of all things is green,'
says the Arab philosopher Haly.

Pollen analysis proves it. Even
in the night the green comes over.

At midsummer, the vernal equinox,
only one wavelength is visible.

But what of the colours we know
as love; the urge to fall asleep

inside the carapace? Stepping close,
the light cuts understanding,

our skins condense dismay.
We face each other wordlessly,

papering over the cracks the way
we use words to paper over

the joins between things. Not that
things are joined but held apart

by *the idea of things*, which brings us back
to words themselves, the way

they oscillate like the movements
of a child's puzzle, shifting tiles one by one

until a pattern is formed—ships
in a sudden & luminous calm.

You know, I like boats. I see
sea-green and it's the deep I want.

Cavatina

'How imperceptibly we become ourselves.'
—CHARLES WRIGHT

Yesterday unfolds tomorrow with today's hands,
draining into the blue—a shifting land
where feeling most at home approaches
stillness. Evaporating mildly in the shallows,
or drifting like fine snow, I am just a visitor.
Beach deposits crumble under brilliant stars,
a montage of blocks along the barren strip
feigning death like stranded fish.

A second coastline starts beyond the first;
this frozen sea of light at the sound's edge.
One thing is clear, the moment won't last long
high on the shore: night after night it comes,
approaching the land as though it's ablaze,
cruising narrow cliffs under waning moons,
revealing life stories baked to sinews in the high
strand's wake, like driftwood cast along the littoral.

Bells ring for a second time this evening
marking some significance or, simply,
to remind between the peals that we are called
to things—wherever things may be—as if to ask me
Who I am? What I am? Where I'm going?
We know who we are. We are who we are
the day we are born, spend the rest of our lives
becoming someone else, like rocks in rising tides.

The Lute Girl's Lament

(after Po Chu-Yi)

By night and by the riverside goodbyes were spoken
but no guitar, no flute was heard.
Words of cold farewell beneath the bright
moon above the body of the stream.

Beneath the maples' flower-like leaves
the river branched and, where the maples ended,
the river began a new world of level country
stilled by the grip of frost.

In the exact moment when
the rest was silence,
Host forgot to go, Guest lingered on,
but no guitar, no flute was heard.

And so I laughed myself from year to year
and the red skirts of song were stained with wine,
but like the torrent the music was lulled
and dark greeted the paling constellations.

Shakkei

Japanese: 'borrowed scenery'; a window framing a distant landscape.

The Myth: A woman frees some captured birds. She is later rescued from a riverbed by swallows that carry her back to earth.

I. A Body of Water

A body of water,
of rivers & lakes
lying in the geographic heart.

The bank trees turning,
each oak & hazel etched
against an evening sky,

their central roots
that find deep levels,
expanding over meadows

and monopolizing streams.
Life has changed
the supporting land:

"One moment I stood
at the river's edge; the next
I was swept away

like letters chalked
on the hull of a boat
stuck on the estuary flats."

II. She Turned Into the River

She turned into the river
as a cloud turns into rain,
her last few moments spread

across the wide alluvial plain,
like the leaves of windswept
willows on the river's edge . . .

bud-burst to mouse ear,
mouse ear to full blade,
late blossom petal fall.

III. Wintering Underwater

'Swallows winter underwater.'
—THE ARCHBISHOP OF UPPSALA, 1555

Beginning to end has begun.
Now streams and deep marshes
sustain migratory breaths

fluctuating seasonally. The river
has reached a denouement—
this daily up & down stuff.

How do they know when it's time
to go and sleep where
water laps? The map says

where they are; the compass
the direction. Here swallows
gather and meanings grow,

the banks in patterns of flux,
learning the waters and waiting
beneath until Spring. On the surface

shadows of willow trees dance
to celebrate remembered ground.
Deep down, the swallows sleep.

IV. *Shakkei*

The light moves north.
Dawn draws across the horizon.
A saturated woman walks back into history.

Shaping the site, she places herself
in the landscape, fleshing it out in the mind—
a dense stand of maple,

each branch the idea of a sacred grove
near a stream where birds drink.
There are only two seasons: Desire & Return.

V. *The Air is Full of Mountains*

The air is full of mountains,
screaming clouds—an orange mist
that sings as a Kabuki actor sings.

Passing over the lip, the air recites
the different names of plants
and birds—willows, swallows—

naming the land on which we stand;
names, names falling on the head
as so much rain falls.

from *The Wanderer's Prayer*

I.

The Footsteps of God is the mythical spot where the river leaves the mountains on its long and varied journey over land towards the sea. Woodland channels, barrages and buildings rise riparian. Walkways bridge these peopled plots.

A god left the soles of his feet pressed in the rocks and that's why people gather here and candles float downstream to drums & music. Leave your shoes by the door, leave your feet by the door, drink and dive and light a candle. We are here to see what we can never see and are ourselves, in doing so, seen—

> sightseer, holy man, beggar-man, priest
> swannee whistler, drink stall holder
> women selling rice balloons

—a multitude at the water's edge, to drink, to bathe, to swim, to pray, to ask for health and a life that moves . . .

and as light fades and the sun stops sun-ness, priests swing incense burning brands, ring gongs & bells and inner space expands to fill the head with earth-fire-water-sky, the air, the sounds that air can hold

> a
> m o
> m e n t

   & the crowd begin singing
    & people dive in
     & all the candled boats embark
      & set off on the swirling eddies
       & buying a boat, we remove our shoes
        & go down to the river's edge
        & by the side   we stop
        & enter with our feet
        & wash our foreheads
       & our hands
       & think of family
      & friends
       & push the fragile vessel out
       & watch it disappear

this little *Ulysses* of a prayer on its roundabout tour to and from
its origins.

II.

The morning's open, random light
falls on *The City of Dreadful Night*.
Rising with the blanket smog, names on names,
a pantheon of scientists & poets:

Calcutta has just thrown up a street named *Shakespeare*,
Kipling, Thackery, the family *Tagore*, Rabindranath's *Gitanjali*
and one more Nobel Prize for the man who found out
the mosquito's secret—Sir Ronald Ross.

This is the oldest culture left on Earth.
It's only right to think about these scientists & poets;
physicists who are now getting into black holes,
getting into Tao; about its pantheistic masses

living in the chaos, its all too human lot—the ever-present
sound of singing "rituals bring us closer to god".

III.

Voices ascend the slippery shore—
this tomb in the seaweed's fetters.
We need only praise
the starfish for constancy.

Silence adorns these islands' coasts
with fugitive joys in huts & palm trees.
The waking fish are snagged
from a tide carving papery neaps

and colonise the olive dullness
wallowing where Hosannas once pulsed.
The wave shadows. The thirst persists.
We leap along lost boulevards of trees.

IV.

A squad of uniformed shy girls,
with coloured pie-sliced parasols,
stir the day back to simplicity.
Their colours gel and twist in time,
trying to dance in synchrony
to *Roll Out The Barrel* on the grass
between a marble monument
to the Raj and a shit-filled ditch.
They miss their steps. They're honest kids.
They're in rehearsal for something big.

The market too has flowers.
I study its narrowing alleys.
Stray dogs run between the banks
of blooms and butchers' slabs in front.
We pass one dog by, skin peeled off
the bone. Eyes out. Agog. A sweet,
sickening smell on the pavement
outside Ronald Ross' malaria lab.
On the wall, his epitaph: 'I find thy
cunning seed, O million murdering death.'

NOTES: The title of the poem comes from *The Odyssey*, Book V. The whole
poem cycle begins on the River Ganges at *Haridwar*, Northern India. *The
City Of Dreadful Night* is Kipling's Calcutta. Rabindranath Tagore's *Gitanjali:
Song Offerings* are free verse recreations of his Bengali poems, modelled on
devotional Indian lyrics, that won the Nobel prize for literature. *Sir Ronald
Ross* was also awarded the Nobel Prize for his discovery that the female
mosquito was the carrier of the malaria virus. Ross was also a poet. 'I find
thy cunning seed, O million murdering death', comes from his poem about
his discovery.

'What We Think of as Home'

'Because what we think of as home is a hazard to others . . .'
—JOHN BURNSIDE, from 'Settlements'

I lived for more than twenty years
with my husband & sons
in Jiangsu Province—

the black terrace under
the white magnolias;
the arcane laws of *feng shui.*

Now I sit between morello trees
suffused in the past
and the vanished.

Pausing at the rotting windows,
there is the familiar. Time
still forms the tasks that keep me here.

Nowhere else do I feel I belong
as I do here. Dawn is still an hour away.
These winter nights linger and linger . . .

Autumn, Mount Fuji

Temporarily is ours the life—having a good time out there in the
hills, eating all that remains of summer's berries. But the days,
the days are short. And the nights? The nights are chill. By morn-
ing, new snow lies all around. Look,
                                        the maple leaves,
already they crimson on the branches.

II

'Get with someone you can trust with tears, with anger and wonderment and utter silence. Get that part done—the sooner the better.'

—THOMAS LYNCH, from *The Undertaking.*

A Poem of Gifts

(for Molly May)

'. . . *por el amor, que nos deja ver a los otros como los ve la divinidad*'
'. . . *for love, which lets us see others as the godhead sees them*'
—JORGE LUIS BORGES, 'Another Poem of Gifts'

I want to give thanks for the garden
    already in bloom this March
    as I sit here with you, curled
    like an aleph in your papoose;
for the balsam of your chatter
    echoic and fluid,
    like an elver in the wash;
for the flexion of your tongue
    throwing muscular vowels
    into the fuzz of sun & dew
    like the musical chimes of a gamelan;
for the brouhaha of the blackbird
    as it picks at a red berry
    or last winter's lingering
    hips & haws;
for the synod of starlings
    gathered in the oak;
for the peony's growth
    we can almost hear
    surging through the soil;
for my dibber pushing through the clod
    to sow the seed that promises blue
    borage at the bottom of the plot;

for the bubble of the acorn
    exploding underground;
for the dewlaps on cattle
    chewing cud in the fields beyond,
    their calves impatient
    at their udders;
for the kazoo of insects
    busy at the nectaries
    of cowslips & daffodils;
for the fresco of morning;
for the whole gamut & hex of Spring;
for your mother
    in her workshop
    unloading the kiln;
for the hubbub & jabber
    of her radio;
for the hoop of love
    that rolls on
    with no beginning
    and no end;
for the unknowable nuances
    of change;
for the nub of pleasures
    which elude me;
for the koan of *Why?*;
for the ingots of your eyes;
for the honey of your dribble;
for your *tabula rasa*.

The Bee Charmer

My father understood them as Rimsky understood—
their vibrant, wavering buzz; their social order.
He was a master charmer, could locate a swarm
of wild bees by lying on his back out in the woods,
his ears down low in spikes of sedge, or purpling florets
of *Yorkshire Fog*
                 and there he'd wait and listen for
the swarm; could hear them coming long before he saw
their beeline to a nearby trove of nectar-laden flowers.
Then he would follow them through the trees to home
and plunder the ingots of their dripping combs.

Colour Theory

He came down one Sunday to a Fauvist's heaven,
chauffeured along the asphalt grey lane
in a turquoise taxi, listening to blues songs,
through dense swathes of pink campions,
iridescent beds of bluebells,
white and nodding parsley umbels,
buttercups, and sulphur-yellow primroses,
stitched into the earth like a kilim.

Along the hedges white ransom sprays and flecks
of starbright shone sharp as a welder's arc
fixing us in the amber sunlight like ancient insects—
the brimstone butterflies were out—as Angel Eyes
observed us and you, copper-haired, said:
'The shadows between the blades of grass *are* red.'

Verres Luisantes

I'm sitting in a lecture in invertebrate zoology,
learning the mating habits of the beetle genus
Lampyris, whose wingless females emit a light
from the end of their abdomens—illuminated *Sirens*;

or someone somewhere is reading out the poem
'Glow Worms'; or the garden I am standing in
is suddenly lit by the candles of glow worm tails
(how can we know which way the memory works?)

when suddenly I'm sixteen again, lying close
to an unforgettable *Française*, on top of Carnac's
giant standing stone, our tips alight like beacons

and I can taste the garlic on her lips—taste a woman
for the very first time—while a sea of glow worms
lures us in below, in the brilliant attractions of sex.

Slippage

(for Tom: 'The rent is do'.)

A dark blue hourglass on the bookshelf fills
with evening light. I turn it over, watch
the sand slip through its waist, narrow as a wasp's
and count the time it takes the sand to fall . . .

Outside, the Western Ocean cracks its whips
against the stacks of rock at Castle Point,
those hulking blocks of limestone that once slipped
into the sea, now ground to sand & quartz.

Inside, the *Irish Theological*
informs us there are two types of slipped disc—
'Hard' & 'Soft'. The first hits suddenly,
the other's slow, like the changes of our love.

Kept indoors by the rain our daughter laughs.
She points out to the bay and voices 'blue'
and I can't help but feel that we're the halves
the sand of her young life now trickles through.

The Trust Territory

I. *If I tell you . . .*

If I tell you your love is a spider's web,
I mean that in its tensile sense—
the strongest substance known to man,
weight for weight tougher than steel.

'Web', I mean, in its tensile sense,
but also with a hint of *home*:
weight for weight tougher than steel,
a place for the creature to rest.

And with that hint of *home*,
a place that gathers morning dew;
a place for the creature to rest,
amazing a passing child's eye.

A thing that gathers morning dew,
my love, is a spider's web,
amazing a passing child's eye.
Please don't take offence—I do not mean

your love is a spider's web
and I the struggling fly.
No, please don't take offence—I do not mean
you are the spider who turns

on me, poor struggling fly.
If I tell you your love is a spider's web,
you are not—repeat *not*—the spider who turns
to feast on the head of her mate.

No, I mean . . . 'the strongest substance known to man.'

II. *I imagine you've changed little* . . .

I imagine you've changed little since our *thing*
in the Great Rift, so far away this morning
as I sit here drinking coffee on the terrace of the café
    La Délicieuse.

I imagine you still wear that face all other
men could love. I am tempted to believe, however
briefly, that although there is no antidote
    there's hope—

the feeling that we've lived through this before
and know what's coming next. Your silence is
obscure. Still you're
    imprisoned

by a world where things are held by threads—
the prince on the princess's hair; Damocles' sword;
all those feelings you shored-up,
    but never fully expressed.

III. *Koi Carp*

This pollen-honeyed evening
your parting gift of Koi carp
rise to the gilded surface.

They flash their dog-brown eyes
beneath the pond's lens;
twitch a muscle and disappear.

But tight in the kernel
of night, they cut through
the dream's meniscus,

stirring the pool's surprises:
quick insects; slow molluscs
down in the muck & the silt.

IV. *Waking in Manhattan*

The night that raised my hopes now whittles down
our options. The morning's heavy snowfall
consumes the blue masses of skyscrapers
and builds on our distance. I open the grille;
imagine us both—exiles on far shores—
staring past the smuts on our windows.
There are patterns in the bird tracks on the ledge.
I fill my eyes with their secret language:
the text of our future; the novel of our love.
All I ask today is you & I rise above
this interval in the theatre of weather,
but I am restless beneath a drift of lies,
blocking light from the glass. I retrieve the dull
hammer of my self and nail the window shut.

V. *da Capo*

da capo / Mus: *'repeat from the beginning'*

You scan the line of albums, lick your lips
and ease one out. It opens in your palm.
Wetting a finger you shuffle through the pages
like a teller. A smile fields your face:

'You see, I'm right,' you say (again).
'It *was* here. You *must* remember—
'our naked bodies joined together;
'warm breezes shaking perfume

'from the clover?' Why is it, I wonder,
I don't recall a thing; but you—oh you!—
your memory is so sharp? You slide it back.
We go to bed. Stare at the ceiling; our latest books.

VI. *December*

Convinced it is a good idea, we spend
the long, dark nights unloading ourselves.
We watch each other twist and bend.

Such a weight of 'this & that' my friend:
each night we pull confessions from the shelves
convinced it is a good idea and spend

the nights awake. Where will this honesty end?
Too late, the old advice not to dig and delve
too deep; we watch each other twist and bend.

Resigned to the damage we may never mend
we drive the clock past Ten. Eleven. Twelve,
convinced it is a good idea. We spend

hours addressing the nightmare of 'The End',
cling tight together, like digger's hand to helve
and watch each other twist and bend.

Once more we see there's nothing *really* to defend.
Perhaps the answer lies in making love?
Unconvinced it is a good idea, we spend
ourselves, watching each other twist and bend.

VII. *Daybreak*

Day breaks with the iridescence
of beetles. Last night remains

a beautiful, desolate thing:
me, lying

like an insect on a silver pin,
waiting for something to happen,

as if the world was about
to reach out

with the answer and you, leaving,
hiding your smile—that thing

you do as much as with
your eyes as with your lips.

Alone, I come-to to this
clock of exquisite sadness.

VIII. *A Breath from the Wood*

Why she appeared in the ruffled beards
of lichen on the trees outside my window,
asking was I now prepared to love,
or just go on pretending, I could not say.

Instead, I sat ashamed of my own breath
and stammered pointless words
about the only options left to us
the whole of the woodwind day.

IX. *I stood before you . . .*

I stood before you, lost for words,
the bunch behind my star-lit back.

'Silence, that's what flowers are,' you said,
'or rather, *a man's way of silencing.*'

X. *Song for the Siren*

The rain is light. Light falls.
A handstroke of sun tans
the sky's western edge.

You sit in the meadow
by a solitary oak, your feet
dipped in a stream of fish

and frogs, your head among
a cloud of flies, crying;
tears that gleam like acorns.

The Vanishing

(two disappearances, for Amanda Dalton)

I.

Deciphering the gnosis of your in-tray,
tacitly you sat for years, but finally slumped,
evaporating from house & firm. Later—
when you botched your fast-lane jump
and they zipped you back to the flat diorama
of the city, fazed & foetid in the pyjamas
you hadn't changed for weeks—their questions
bounced from the pink wall of your stare:
'Let's try again: who, why, what, when, where?'

200 miles from home the police bring in
a woman: 'Disturbing the peace'. Homeless,
nameless, no next of kin. 'Unusual, yes,'
you apparently agree, picking at your cuticle,
nor more concerned by anything than by a broken nail.

II.

The sun slashes out at corrugations
on the tin roof of the gamekeeper's shed.
Grasses shoot sharp pollens up his nostrils.
The hedges shimmer in their floral suits.
Beneath the fallen limbs of oak & ash,
museums of fern & moss hide out
making calculations of the air—how far
they may safely fling their spores. Cock
pheasants bark a harsh tattoo as, silently,
he ties another crow's corpse to the gibbet—
blackness of folklore; woody voodoo.
In a patch of disturbed greenery, the humus
lies full of nerves: the attentions of woodlice
and worms rearranging the misunderstood.

At the River *Odet,* on Max Jacob Bridge

I'd like to hold you here,
     at a distance,
so close I might yet touch you,
but still   *Over There,*
       under the magnolias,
their fallen petals
                like angels in flight,
as you cross the River *Odet*
on Max Jacob Bridge,
the rain misting gently.

Pedestrians glide
            to bars nearby,
inhabiting spaces
                somewhere outside
their own soft murmurings.

These are the days;
the river lined
by peeling
       London Planes,
the mottle of their bark a map
of where we might arrive
as we become the *Why*
of where we are.

The moment is everything
beautiful.
     The river low,
         flowing under

a sudden drop of sun;
these little boys & girls you see;
those old men & women;
every one a part of it.
They are the same river.

Tonight the current is quick,
a liquid membrane
of eddying light
washing you into
the waters behind
                    my eyes;
the old, cluttered
canal of my love.

Other rivers may flow by,
flow *into* our lives,
taking us back
to our natal streams,
but this littered stream is purer
isn't it; distilled?
            something to do with
emptying ourselves,
because nothing is bigger
than the nothing we have;
or the source it has come from,
            returns to.
Even the reflected stars
invoke it.

Winter into Spring

(for Lee Harwood)

'Summer of course follows. There is no
winter in my world.

Perhaps as you read this poem
you will be pleased, and the smile of
memories and hopes will come into your face.

I do hope this happens as it's the first
time I've written nature poetry.'
                    —LEE HARWOOD, from 'Pastoral'

~

Land is all in the belonging
but, for now, belonging lies
in limbo,
            bone hard beneath
a gauze of mist.
Each grass blade
                crusted stiff;
great skating pools
in rutted gateways;
                the gates
rodded with ice.

In the hedge's lea,
                frost
until late afternoon,
where the sun cannot reach.

The slow impasto of snow.

My breath plumes,
      past leafless orchard,
            solid duckpond,
the ideogram of the empty
dovecote.
        Exhausted,
you sleep
      in this snow-
storm of my making.

No one tired as you
can read the wind.

. . . Sleep greens the world . . .

    ⁓

The days don't turn light until eight.
Darkness falls by mid-afternoon,
the hours between, a dim twilight.
The only colours:
              witch-hazel;
yellow-bright clumps of gorse bushes;
purple straps of brambles coursing
hedges; patches of dried red sedge;
the russet fronds of dead bracken.

Buried under cloaks of last year's
leaves,
        the new crosiers unfurl.

Pheasant cocks possess the dark lanes,
their white collars bright against red

necks—gewgaws on the dull linen
of winter. Along the river,
the only sounds the slip & slop
of water in ripples; the cries
of hungry birds.
                    Starling flocks swoop
in bubbles. Crows pick carrion.
Plump dun doves peck at wooded floors.
Nutting squirrels strip trees of bark
where no beech mast or filberts are.

The ice, at last, has gone. "Sorry."
Being here with you—observing—
like looking through the end of one
small experience and finding
it makes *everything* look bigger.

          ∾

Dormant February. This love is
not some experimental station
we use only to look into ourselves.
On thin hazel tips:
                    catkins.
Ash straplings
              black budded.
Mary's Tapers & daffodils.
Dog's mercury,
violet,
        gorse
            & primrose.

Last year's beech leaves
clinging on like smiles;
like "memories & hopes".

⁓

The weeks of crows & doves? Over.
Songbirds return—
                    blackbirds, blue-tits,
robins & fieldfares;
                    goldfinches
picking last season's teasel heads;
all exercising larynxes.

A green woodpecker hammers out
his territory's bounds. At dusk,
moon-eyed owls wing hedges hunting.
Squirrels pursue other squirrels.
On the air the stink of fox scats.
Badgers emerge to musk.
                Under
the ground,
                    their supine mates give birth.

"Birds choose their mates
                this month, my love . . ."

⁓

April is the cuckoo's month. "Cuckoo".
When days stretch out at both ends—
the sun sooner risen and late-setting—
rashes of ladybirds settle on nettles.

Mornings: brimstone moths—
asterisks on the script of dawn.
Evenings: flies in clouds
        over scrubby lanes,
their legs dangling,
                like sprites.

Through hedgerow & bank,
cleavers struggle;
bumblebees & caterpillars—
exponential as Fibonacci—
hum, buzz and munch.
Wood ants & spiders
build nests; webs.
                Birds & bees
tap dandelion sap.
                Goldfinches
strip the floss of their seeds.
Mushrooms under the birches.
Mole fortresses.
Doe hares raising leverets,
        safe from stoats,
                from buzzards, foxes . . .

[a hawk strikes its prey
                and soars away].

Beech & ash budburst.
        Sweet smell of bluebells.
                The salmagundi of a copse in spring.

The yoo-hoo & yammer
of blackbirds & goldcrests;
           nuthatches, jays;
                yaffles.

The first badger cubs
emerge
           from their setts at night
to mewl at the albumen moon.

The first leaves of apples.

       ∾

We brush our hands
along spikes of king ferns;
shower ourselves in fern dust—
make ourselves invisible—
at once a part of the wood,
visible only to ourselves;
each other;
                happily
somewhere in between
shadow & light.

       ∾

May greens itself.
                Thunder
rolls in from the coast
settling over our wet plain.
The river high & swollen
where the droughts of summer
leave slow, shallow pools.

Fords overflow;
　　　　　the river bursts,
flooding fields—
　　　　　fish stranded
in grass where the waters recede.

Courting snipe flit the bogs.
Songbirds raise their fledglings.
Bats skim the surface of the pond.
Night frogs calling.
　　　　　Together
we watch Maybugs
　　　　　smudge themselves
against our windows,
drawn to our night lights.

Here is the fire talking.
　　　　Here are healing rituals.
　　　　　Here is an offering

of two pairs of shoes
　　　　together at the door—shoes
　　　　　in place of where we were.

　∼

Coda

'I try again to summarise
our journey,'
　　　　Winter into Spring.
Between ice
　　　　and the unknown

shemozzle beyond,
we hold our breath.

To understand at all, is to trust
the capital of our memories
and they have long since been
engulfed
            by the rot of the woods;
the stramash and shindig
of wildness
                as all cities finally will.

Yet perhaps we're still there—
lovely, illogical place!—
climbing the jutting crags
of our dreams;
cushioned by laughter;

by our desire to stay
        but be gone
                in a moment;
by the world—
        each other—
                our sublime habit.

Roadkill

The squirrels are nutting in zigzags.
Along the lane they flit before the car
like particles in Brownian motion,
trying to conceal the drey's location;
the winter hoard. Their suicidal runs
recall the corpse I found last week
on the same soft verge and discovered
(whilst teasing the skull apart from spine)
that the cat was *ours*, somehow *larger*
in death, bloated by gas, her bowels,
her eyes & anus eaten out by grubs.

I wanted her bones for the ossuary;
wished to bleach the marrow of her brain
in a bucket or bowl, to join the bones
of garnered birds & foxes. And yet
when I came back with the spade
to split her skull's white rose from
its brittle stem, her corpse was gone:
buzzard meat . . . or might I just expect
to meet her back at home, sitting on
the cobbles in the backyard; waiting
patiently in the sun for my return?

Chess Moves

After the passionate debates are over
about us doing what is right, or not,
we make our way back to the heart,
or what we call 'the heart' but mean
as somewhere *other* within us, near
the border of where we are and where
we'd like to be—
                          but just as chess moves
gain their meanings later in the game,
we find the heart is sometimes missing
and have to stand behind the things
we said—as one would stand behind
a low-score poker hand, or throw of dice—
facing each other, staring at our feet,
wondering if we're rooting in the dust?

The Broken Mould

I.

The broken mould conforms in its own way
like the streets & piazzas of a great
metropolis buzzing with shock waves by day
and yet when all subsides little more remains
than the dream of tomorrow's wage
and the debt we owe the past but only pay
by packing up our things and going away.

II.

As the sun's white disk begins to fade
we walk to the twisting beat of waves.
On the top of a cliff by the wind's grace
we watch two boys skimming stones all the way
out to the groynes. Their pebbles seem to say:
'We know exactly where the spray
will rise where next we land'. We stop and pray.

III.

God: we have one chance in two. Those may
seem good odds, but they can change,
for no one wants to live inside *His* shade.
What we seek devotedly in the failing
light begins to wear away. We fish all day
with little luck; play conspiratorial games;
slam our counters down so the table shakes.

IV.

We catch ourselves in another fray;
wait each other out for hours. No way
either of us is going to give way.
'This is pointless,' you finally say,
raising a stir, troublingly real. You may
be right. Then your face begins to break
into smiles; keeps my loneliness at bay.

An Old Cartoon

The sun unwinds itself from night's monsoon.
It is as if we've slept in separate beds
and yet I wake to the imagined smile
behind your sleeping face, tired of being
alone, or rather, welcoming the small,
everyday acts that raise their heads
again & again in cheerful tones, flickering
in stop-start frames, as in an old cartoon.

It takes all day to reach the other *us*,
the truthful one that lies beneath the surface
of this game. Our hope lies in the scripts
we read and in our reading gathering hints
of what lights up the paper from inside:
for love's a lantern . . . and isn't it burning bright?

III

'We are living in times that might perhaps be called *The Dark Ages with Irony.*'

—BILL TALEN, in *The Ecologist*

A Life Story

'As she laughed I was aware of becoming involved in
her laughter and being part of it, until her teeth were
only accidental stars with a talent for squad-drill.'
    —T.S ELIOT, from 'Hysteria' in *Prufrock* (1917)

An old lady is telling us the story of her life. From her rattan chair
she removes the cable-knitted cosy from the pot and serves us tea.
She speaks of her first marriage at the age of sixteen. Her husband
died tragically of an untreatable illness the following year and she
married again at twenty. She says she began smoking in 1920 and
has puffed through a packet a day for eighty-three years. She
smokes a good deal while she's talking, but she doesn't inhale.

What holds her here? Tea. Cigarettes. The past mostly; the past
and a few relationships. Continuity of heart, she also says, which
lives alongside memory. How much memory? Let us investigate the
documents of her date of birth; baptismal and church records;
age at marriage; time until the birth of her children; the present
ages of her offspring. According to her account, her father died at
a hundred; her mother at a hundred and two. She had seven broth-
ers and sisters, but she is the only survivor. Her son from her second
marriage was born when she was twenty-nine and is now seventy-
nine. We do the maths:

> Twenty-nine and seventy-nine makes her one hundred
> and eight.

She was married for the second time at only twenty, ten years after
the outbreak of the First World War, which began eighty-nine years
ago now. Again we do the maths:

> Twenty plus eighty-nine minus ten. Now she's ninety-nine.

We know she started smoking in 1920, when her younger brother died at the age of twenty, from a wound sustained during the Great War. He was seven years older than she.

Eighty-three plus twenty minus seven makes her ninety-six.

Her second husband, who was five years younger than she, died some twenty-eight to thirty years ago aged seventy-five. We work it out:

Twenty-nine plus five plus seventy-five makes one hundred and nine.

I myself have never been good at ages and find her impossible to gauge; she changes age by the minute! We drink our tea and realise that no one, not one of us, knows which of her truths is true. What is more we realise, no one, not even she, cares.

The Wedding / The Elegant Rooftops

I hope I don't start crying again. Ever since the kids were born I cry at anything, the palette of emotions tracking me for days like balloons.

Balloons float up next to us, over the elegant rooftops, decorating the monotone slate like confetti on a driveway after the wedding party's over.

The musicians for a final time take up their instruments—noble, durable—and the wedding party's once more in full-swing; everyone believing in the players' notes that pop out of nowhere like confetti from the sky, only to disappear again as fragments in a dream.

They always knew their score, this pair. Met by chance in a city park; lay down together reading books in depths of green. I say 'by chance', but I was inadvertently responsible. We always are. And soon they sang with a single tongue—their special vanity.

Often there is no sun—only an indeterminate light; light and the voices of wind—over the elegant rooftops. Or sometimes a trickle of water, like a confused smattering of tongues in the overcrowded suburbs; their grey pyramidal summits occupying the sky the way the inner life occupies men & women: their windows facing shaded courtyards, where couples commingle amicably, and other tired & lonely guests brokenly wander.

And in the early dawn, as the sun & moon regard each other a moment; outside teahouses & night cafés on wide & empty streets that own themselves completely until the bright hours; everyone returns home, together or alone it doesn't matter much, happy simply to live in themselves after yesterday's affirmations, under the gentle droop of the elegant rooftops.

Triptych

I. *An Ill Wind*

On a city terrace rooftop, a yellow windsock spins in desultory breezes. It slips its hitch, stabs the sky and from the squall descends into a Judas Tree's bare branches.

Two men stare through their half-frosted window; argue who should go and fetch it down; wonder if either will ever step out once more into the gusting world.

II. *Japonica. Arum*

They say *the quince* and not the apple was Eden's first and last temptation, which Adam took from Eve to eat, sensing how she knew it was *sweeter* than the apple and surely ready to drop.

As they exit Paradise in mourning Arum Lilies sprout where Eve's tears fall.

III. *The Covenant*

According to the Tuareg *marabout*, young Ham defied old Noah's rule: "Man shall not *know* animals on the Ark."

Below Mount Ararat the herds arrive, from long migration, huddled & defensive; keeping out the men with wire fences.

Life in *Ultima Thule*

The pastor's nasal monotones evoked a stair-step pattern hatched in black, shadowing the ceaseless flow of air outside our windows. As his sermon continued I ducked beneath the pedal organ's metal pipes, past font & screen and out of church to test the resonance of sky—the cries of owls—slinking across the jagged steppes with their sculptures of ice, their monoliths marked with the subtle inscriptions of lovers surrendering to the kiss of salt & rain.

You were sitting on the menhir, waiting . . .
beneath high buttes, the empty plains, expanses of birch & pine trees chilled by winds that cut beyond redemption. There we felt the translucent walls of day accept us in their languorous way; the new directions the old was taking focusing our hearts on ourselves.

'Think the farthest thought!' you cried in some attempt to heave ourselves away, but the reverse would soon be true I thought; the village would return to dust, as we sat there in our hearts, admiring the inconsistencies of scenery from the caves of our passion, red with the scoria of mistakes we've made.

Inside, his love-thy-neighbour sermon ended.

'There's certainly plenty of trust,' you said—the love in your eyes giving nature a nudge—'just mostly in the wrong places.'

The Year Before we Were Healed

. . . we journeyed here to orient ourselves to Earth's magnetic field, to try and survive at great depths; to be luminescent like plankton.

Below our windswept rise, the estuary's rivers joined as one; our worries put by for a moment.

The elements pressed in, as if reclaiming the idea of themselves in the minds of walkers. In a silence we tuned from the wind, we fused ourselves with the under-cliffs; became like fossil corals pushing through time.

"To stand on this same spot where men & women have always stood, wondering; rooted in the textures of the sea," you said, touched by a melancholy wildness.

A bicyclist bisected the shoreline.

Some winches groaned and hawsers tightened—two sailboats putting out to sea. I held a prayer firmly in my mouth as we trudged back through sea-wrack, the cold sea-spray a reason for urgency.

At the bottomless beachhead tunnel, we scratched our initials in sandstone: our rough glyphs joining the fading signatures of sailors; parted limpits . . .

The Hydroaktylopichharmonica

With the death of the author I hesitate to enter her story, but it proves irresistible; there lies her pen and here am I in the burgeoning exurbs, just itching for something to do.

Look, her doorway! I have often passed her door before, but never have *seen* it 'til now. The rain describes diagonals on my iris. A chink of light describes her open door. Now there's a good excuse—let's venture inside and see what she has left us in her will . . .

Is this a house or a museum? Its faultless proportions and deep porticoes suggest the latter. Notice especially the row of large glasses displayed in the sash window—the hydroaktylopichharmonica!—and there is someone, *the semblance of a figure,* playing them. Can it be the spirit of the author?

The apparition wets a finger; runs its pad around the tumblers' rims. In gently ringing tones the glasses respond: Weeeee-ooooo-eeeee. She returns their tune with delightful 'traas' & 'laas' & 'tums'; a spectral song. Her eyes are some rare and undiscovered element; her fingertips, trembling needles.

How this angel sings!
> Her song is the rain's hearse.
> Heaven is where her ribs rise.

Shooting the Sun

The coastal path directs us like a telepath: our cross-staff & astro-labe. Like apprentice mariners *shooting the sun*, it leads us out from sweet to brackish; to ozone & salt-spray. From shoals in shining waters to the intricate grain of the coast, everything happens with deceptive ease. On shore, the fishing rods tremble; their quivers meaning bites.

Birds—I think they're fulmars aren't they?—bank on high winds, the shirr of their wings in a soundless sky. Sea grasses flex. Waxen figures bob in a boat with a sail. Old wooden cabins line the water-front. High on the strand, the dry remains of dogfish twist in piles of weed. Big & busy bugs skim over meres behind the dunes, both-ering cattle & sheep. A bird's song cascades up-shore, carried by wind to the geese at rest on the reed banks. Buds of poppies, mallow & clover; swallows plucking insects from the surface. Ducks fan the ripples; waders stilt from foot to foot. A heron, motionless, startled by apparent nothingness, sweeps into the stillness of the sky. Its sudden, guttural cry. Slash of a sinuous fish sliding through dark waters.

Clouds sluice across the sky like tea in a Wedgwood cup.

A fish carcass draws a harrier down. It flies low, dipping feet into water; the bobbing fish belly-up. Claws gaff and lift. Downstream, its flight path gently curved, the hawk descends. A walker's dog disturbs the feed. The hawk forgets its quarry. The dog moves in, licks the fish, then pulls off at the walker's distant voice. Among alder & birch the morning takes place: the leaps & bounds of forag-ing foxes; mute deer laying back their ears. Above, clear space and enveloping light; the sea in our wings.

Celebration of an unseen bird.

Minutely   over the flats   the tide.

Blue-Tits

(for Laurie, years from now)

The children are building sun castles. I am sitting with them in the garden watching the blue-tits build a new metaphor.

Fine day though it is, primrose-dotted the twisting reaches of the hedges withhold something from us—all that damn mystery!

Memory is a little nest; a balanced interweaving of desire; the dialogue of what we remember and how. The tension strung between them.

The children start their tugging at either end of a toy neither truly wants. The forgotten and the need to be recalled fight it out.

The blue-tits work to the rhythm of their chirping: '*Me-mory, me-mory, me-mory*'.

With everything forgotten comes a little death: *Me mori, Me mori, Me mori.*

The children are playing in the garden, caught between desire and memories they don't yet know they have—their need to crack out of the egg, to jump the nest, to fly.

from *Field Notes*

Towards the river's seaward turn the flow is slow, meandering. Wide tidal flats at the sea's low tide support a spread of hungry birds. Silt brought down from inland fans the delta, between the reeds. Here molluscs & crustaceans breed. To the eyes of walkers on sterile dunes, where only the lonely skylark nests in monotonous marram & shifting sand, the estuarine mud-flats seem a bland expanse. But to hungry oystercatchers the casts of worms & clams are treasured finds. They stun their prey with single stabs. Shell duck, eider & avocets scythe the mud. Glutted, they roost inland, waiting for the sea to ebb. Knot flock in thousands where the eel-grass *Zostera* grows. Duck, Dunlin & Brent Geese gather. I note this quietly in my field book . . .

from *The Diary of an Ugly Human Being*

'The thing you have always suspected about yourself the minute
you become a tourist is true: a tourist is an ugly human being.'
— JAMAICA KINCAID, from *A Small Place*

∼

Note: *The 'Diary' is a form of Cento—a collage of lines and*
material from a large collection of 1950s nature magazines.

∼

. . . the wooden houses nodded skyward, beneath the peaks of the
mountain cirque. The village streets were crowded with ducks,
geese & chickens and stalls where women traded figs & peaches, red
& green peppers. Men smoked over coffee, discussing deals & prices.
In a huge leather purse a boy carried a squealing pig.

It was late summer and the grapes were ripening on the shores of
the lake. No simple task to find a guide to take us but, a man
secured, he promised us fields of lush tobacco, stucco villas, olean-
ders & olives. 'You're tourists after all.' Here are no bored guides
with windy lectures.

The guide's truck whined in protest at the grade. Winds soughed
through the cheeses neatly piled in the meadow by his rusted
curing shed. When he cut the engine we all jumped down. Great
earth clods made it difficult to walk uphill, but no one worried;
vines were dropping their clusters in heaped green windrows above
the rocky knuckles and, inside his home, rough dough forced itself
through his wife's firm fingers, as a foretaste of our pleasures. 'It
is hard to grow things here,' she told us, 'but we can coax greenness
from nothing.'

Satisfied with the bread & cheeses in our stomachs, we had never been more relaxed, lazing on the sunny peaks. Birds lapped syrups from the mulberry arbours. Our voices made them disappear like fading rainbows . . .

'Somewhere near here,' our guide told us, 'Legend tells of a river that flows upside down.' He wanted then to take us, but I was all for staying where we were; had never seen more artful fishermen flinging flies in graceful arcs for trout & grayling. What need did we have for his mythology; or the stories of misdemeanours that buzzed around the village? Who was that, anyway, causing all this fuss by dragging History into the present; dredging up Race and Economics and the state of Paradise?

~

That night the little inn was filled with the noise of dice & poker, taught in whistles & whispers by huddles of ancient men. One sign said 'Men' the other 'Ladies'. 'That's the Ladies' bar. By law,' the landlord said.

Here was the slice of entertainment: drink & cards. By the end of that long night they'd taught me everything there is to know about the game: a careful and considered take on chance; to always face the door and trust no novice; how to shine a puddle of a hand.

One old man was still shuffling the pack when midnight called 'Time', long overdue. 'Double or quits to win your pennies back,' he called me. The village held no debts; no credit. 'Wealth is where you find it' seemed their motto. So this is how it goes, I thought, listening to the tick of my coins as they fell into his cup.

~

Every cottage had its loom—a little workroom, excluding the wives from public view, the custom now ingrained. The shops shut-up for evening prayers. These fatalist families high in the hills, whose faith allowed them describe each other by the few possessions of life—an axe, a bandoleer of smuggled ammunition—I watched them touch noses in greeting.

Frontiersmen by nature, many moved with job & season: in summer, fishermen, miners or loggers; men who swung a double-bitted axe as though it were a ping-pong paddle. In winter they hibernated in towns, spending money, visiting wives & children. High wages & overtime pay lured them across the borders. For many on either side of the line, repartition brought not happiness but sorrow—the tragic choice between one's Nation and one's Home.

≈

The people here dislike—despise—the lens. Dark blurs slid back inside their houses when we passed. Conscripts from the local barracks in creased khaki asked me to put my camera down. In four simple words we heard the whole of their philosophy: *You are not I.*

≈

We stopped to show our ID as we crossed the narrow border. Below us precipitous goat tracks gilded the hills with mica-flecked ribbons. Guards in black patent leather were on the look out for guerrillas who hid out in the hills and fell on the towns in covert night time missions. We stopped beside packed transport vans and clusters of crowded cabanes—a prison camp for who knows who?—the faces of men & boys inside black with sleeplessness and journeying. They called to us for news of their villages; their wives & sisters; with sobs in their voices. Their throats were thin from nothing but old soup watered down.

'Our Reception Centres allocate immigrants to suitable occupations as soon as possible,' the guard explained quite curtly. With sundry other passengers we showed him our stamped permits. Even without the curfew our travel would have been limited; confined to the limits of the valley. The guard turned a pale-blue eye on me. In the ground outside his checkpoint, a mirror wedged between the tines of a cleft stick. This was the day he did his shaving.

~

Conspicuous, we found ourselves invited to the headman's house. 'You will stay at my little abode. My mother-in-law snores like an earthquake and my children will drive you mad with their questions, but my wife is the best cook and our beds are soft as clouds.'

As we arrived, he was working an adze down a tree trunk. His wife sang songs whilst washing dirty linen in a hollowed tree. 'Our guests!' she cried and welcomed us inside. The sound of village bells, like cracked buckets, shook the air. They echoed from the hand-split shingles on the roof; its snugly dovetailed logs and chimney topped with a stork nest full of fledglings. The low walls made of local clay and plastered over, the round end faced the east, where Jesus died. Cone-shaped hayricks in the yard. Michaelmas daisies. Apples ripening. The smell of bruised turf where he had been cutting peat, blocks of it, piled up neatly, left to dry. Along the hedges the berries were crimson and, in the brakes of bracken beyond the gate, a flicker of fox caught our eyes. The early evening cool brought on the calls of cardinals. Inside at the table, delicious trout & special oatmeal soup; jugged hare & redcurrant jelly. The headman's wife reported on the weather. Conversation at dinner drifted to the new reports of fighting. 'We devote our lives to making cheeses on the tops of slowly eroding mountains,' he said. 'And why? You know, today, some bandit killed a family on the trail.' He brushed his whiskers dry. 'They drift unobtrusively into our villages and suddenly shoot us down. The safety of our lives is meaningless; our homes are like trodden down anthills. Where's the time to live & celebrate good doings?' I looked down. 'But now is no time for such Englishness!' he laughed, 'taking our pleasure so sadly. Why worry; enjoy what you can! We don't live *in* the past; but *with* it. This is our heritage & delight. Our myths, our art, our civics, our philosophy are one. Our gods are amenable to reason. Drink!'

~

He stared at the walls about us: 'They have seen so much of good & bad,' he said. 'When our neighbouring lands began their threats & actions, we became angry. I took my rifle and put bullets in five of them.' I saw his rifle hung up on the wall, a brass tack in the butt & fore stock for every man he killed. I counted fifty-five. 'They say that when we die and go to Heaven, we make request for bread & cheese and then a rifle. If we cannot get one, we turn around and get out of there!'

'But you have magnificent scenery, fine climate and wonderful soil; everything you need to live well.' He stared at me hard. 'You forget one thing. The land ties us to destiny; to strategy; to grim defence. Many have stormed these mountains' walls: the Persians, the Greeks, the legions of Rome; the Byzantines, your *C'ouer de Lion* Richard; the Lusignan kings of French crusades; the glittering doges of Venice; Turkish plunderers by land, corsairs by sea; the British, Napoleon, Hitler. All nations have swept around these wide plateaus, forcing our peoples up into the hills, here to seek our safety in the rocks. A man who loves his land does not abandon it casually. Ours is a waypoint in history's great processions. First we are Nationals and will fight anyone who says we are not. But I have a Slavic grandmother, Greek ancestors way back. Grandfather speaks German. Magyars, Slovenes, Poles, Czechs, Serbs, Croats, Romanians, Ukrainians, Christians, Moslems, Jews . . . It makes us what we are—a happy confused throng!—like nobody else on earth.'

~

Under a striped awning, the annual mystery play trickled away. They seemed to live their lives by successions of parades, costume fetes, spectacles. Tunes came over from a Regency barrel organ. The louvres on the general store were shut. The owner sat in the dark, refilling cartridge cases.

Everyone was waiting for the verdict on the captured bandit. Flogging was the usual punishment for friends; the enemy, another matter. A sweepstake was based on its outcome. And the town in appetite waited.

~

'Punishment is not a remedy,' I offered. 'It succeeds only in arousing antagonism and defeating one's purpose.'

The headman looked at me, as though the words I offered were rattlesnakes. 'Your wisdom has no place,' he laughed. 'We know you correspondents. There is nothing here to satisfy you but war. Goodbye.'

As the bandit stood in the junta's dock, we regarded each other coolly. It struck me it was no longer clear which of us was on trial.

~

The final day began by the corral. Children ran past in a laughing game of tag, their red cheeks fresh with scrubbing. Adults danced and played the blanket tossing game. A fat & jolly gypsy king sequestered me to join the entertainments. 'Here's a gentle bull; you take a try!' Enthusiastic cries, '. . . so small . . . so young . . . so gentle . . . the bull does you no harm!'

I slipped myself inside the fenced arena. The bull at first ignored me. I took 'the cape' (a ragged scrap) from the village Master of Bulls. 'Wave your little flag!' they chanted. I tried this while the creature pawed the earth. Both of us, it seemed, were gathering courage. He charged; I stood, the safest thing to do. The Bull Master seized me from behind and made me twist. The bull sped past to buffet the fence. Amidst great cheers I walked towards him. The creature turned and charged once more. With a flip I lay flat on my back. The gallery bade me rise from out the dust; my feet would not obey. Remembering the beast was still at bay, I raised myself, disgraced. The bull stood calmly by the fence. 'Such a little bull. . . so gentle. . . ' I heard as I mounted the rails.

～

The entertainments over, the soldiers of the makeshift garrison stood in line at the end of the old corral. The azure of the sky was blanched with heat. In uniform with special insignia, the headman emphasized his words, pointing his finger like a pistol at the peaks. The captured bandit, blindfold, stood silent. No sound broke his final solitude.

The first shots missed and smashed the provost's china shop behind the small arena. The second salvo struck, echoing among the hills, across the scrubby flats.

He dropped, leaving a crouching widow somewhere in the distance, across a border. Behind us, even the mountains look startled.

Old men threw their hats; youths stamped along; old women cried: 'This is the happiest day of my life; now I am willing to die'.

～

Our guide pulled me close and kissed my crown as though we were brothers. 'You want to get away before the real shooting starts,' he said. This is no place to be when the gods begin tossing their weapons. I will find you a letter to smooth the way.'

～

I took my place aboard a mule, like the US cavalry riding to the rescue. Crowds of cheering youngsters. Flowers too flew through the air. Morale was good, men joked and sang. A band followed. 'You must take something with you!' It took me half an hour to persuade them I could not accept. Everyone waved as we rode out of town, offering us company to the stream across the trail.

We came to the stream. I turned to say goodbye. All our newfound friends had vanished. In disappointment, our feet and memories trudged through the roistering brook.

We took a frugal meal; a nose bag lunch. A dozen deer emerged from cover, standing in a grove of young blue pines—we made our way in secrecy, fearful of bandits; while the deer awaited natural deaths. A woodpecker echoed like a tribal drum. Something splashed in the sunlit stream. A creature scuttled through the underbrush, scattering leaves.

We zoomed across the international border, naming wildflowers and pointing out oddities. Evenings, we camped and strummed our old guitar . . .

Events Seem Clear Enough, but . . .

. . . on the first day movement didn't exist. The citizens froze, just as on the icy sandbars cranes were huddling too. Puttering tugs sent struggling wakes. Children were crammed into sanatoria, hotels & youth clubs. Education, the cultural courts—the ratio was getting closer, especially in the language. We ate, sweated and survived; something like devotion reflected in our windows.

To us the dates ran together in calculations that occupied our brains while we conversed—the shapes of ancient phrases, their surfaces polished with use. They seemed to possess their own incandescence, glowing silver, then rose and finally mauve. Looking towards a cityscape—the blue of television sets. How could these all share in the dissolution?

People ashore sometimes saw the glow, a glimpse at what they might have been, painting their houses and building roadside shrines. Local legend recorded marks on every surface of the landscape, naming each place after a body part—"This is London": a lock of hair; a footprint; loose nail clippings. The final influx of the *Olde Worlde* and the story of those who used it.

A rail track led us to the memory of others. Looking for work that wasn't there wasn't the real madness, only a symptom. Leaving, I swung my light across the buildings and along the shoreline, catching the edge of a thousand pieces of brash ice. As I balanced, my sight adjusting, there were the children they'd missed, growing up in the angular eye sockets of each other.

The Sleep Switch

To call them by their real names admits imagination
and intuits the thinking of animals or strangers
speaking the sounds of the answers we seek;
yet what is so unstable and uncertain as the words everyone
    knows?
All things forgetfulness lifts up hang perishable tomorrow,
knowing that time could polish them, writing it all,
abandoned to the rigours of marasmus and escaping
reason, obstinate in the face of memory.

But it is soon blunted, this spell of blindness,
by reciting the signs in sleep. Rotation and mixing
return the words to astonished palates
and allow us to unburden ourselves,
though we know with faith's mysterious certitude
that nobody dreams in words, in gilded capitals.

Fakirs & Yogis with their breathing exercises;
trucks that carry frozen meat,
they each remind us the number of Chosen is fixed,
so where a harvest of silence & darkness
puts an end to this priceless confusion—
to religious ceremonies & devices up our sleeves—
the misfortune of losing faith obscures the need
to lose the soul to save it,
leaving the refuge abandoned by maddening dawn
and rediscovers the path that leads from the other side of the
    face.

All this keeps its hold over the public.
Having come down to the present
we look forward to the models, the opening words & anomalies
that take the form of words, saying nothing
of whole lives in which not a single one figures.
To think it was we who invented those names;
that out there in the world Nothing & Everything is happening.
To think that the mind would fall into the error of believing
the masses of humanity who swarm around it
today bewildered, yesterday forgotten and tomorrow
        unpredictable,
is the understood thing sleeping in the pardonable confusion.

Some Improvements

I.

Moving from snapshot to motion picture a moment sees someone guard their time. The desire to land is understandable: years have gates through which the blurred edges and open shapes of living things adapt to the process of healing from the moment they get up in the morning until the moment they get up in the morning, writing out the details of anxious silence with ritual annotations & imitations that steal the day, receiving our shuffles & cries.

Living there and lying awake the answers sleep and the city collapses, meaning the miracle of outer surfaces is crushed even more powerfully. Afterwards it disappears and this is the force that turns it into the mystery one thousand or more books locked up.

We follow the silent chapters and translate the main qualities of the emotion into a name—the prologue to possessing an unalterable shape. A temporary animal might recognise the difference with dreamy detachment merely by shape & arrangement and alone succeed where home habits let us examine ourselves, the fragments of the words we use, as we see this all again later, life upon life, the apparent tracks leading us back to the main road . . .

II.

It was chiefly a matter of feeling. Friends, filled with the ease of forgetfulness, rotated noises in their ears. But the languor & softness of the blood was a kind of sleep safely delivering opinions to the world with the sterile stroke that comes from the daily routine of nerve centres in the brain.

Nostalgia is ruined when we think. The idea of going back fades, an undesirable dream, but measures the changes over our lives and what did we care so long as we got better? Years are the brief oblivion, the secret incendiaries that living ferments. In our own time we need the stimulus of what is past, but are more interested in our own headaches with an adult's fascination for toys as if warm blood bestowed immortality. We lie at the water's edge awaiting our turn on the pyre while old men dispense folk medicine, solving the problems with nicknames and the little things we learn.

The problem is straightforward—we are all others and cannot even distinguish *Yes* from *No*.

Eventually, they say, a miracle occurs—the doors reopen and the new road winds back to the old city. People said trees wouldn't grow here but look, blossom! and it was true, as far as we could see, the crude walls *were* covered at last in an avalanche of blooms.

IV

The Forger's Epitaph

He did it all in his own name,
but all in others' hands.

An echo's the past in the future.
Here lies an echoing man.

Blindfold Birds

In 1899 Gertrude Bacon wrote an article for *The Strand Magazine* in which she exhibited blindfold drawings of pigs collected from eminent figures of the day. Bacon maintained that, just as hand-writing will reveal certain characteristics of the artist's personality, even more so will the blindfold pig. The same is true of birds. Consider the delusions signified by an overly long beak; the schiz-ophrenia of doubled wings; the melancholy of a down-turned bill; the kleptomania of detailed claws; the obsessions of a torso dense with feathers; the intellect of a beady eye; the absentmindedness of the missing tail; the meditative sketch of an owl drawn in the hollow of a tree; the curiosity of a hen pecking grits on the ground; the diligence of a dipper formed in short, neat lines; the flamboy-ance of an albatross swirling free; the latent violence in the heavily set crow; the desire for oblivion in a diver; the imagination of feath-ers caught in flight etc . . .

This space is for your own blindfold drawing of a bird

This space is for a friend's analysis of your drawing

To All You Squabbling Poets

For everything you've ever said, or thought to do,
      the road take your eye!

May you lie under perpetual malediction, bored to death
      by the monotonous logic of chanting nuns.

May you aim ceaselessly towards your featureless targets;
      be lost forever in an interminable fog, like flies
      trapped inside ping-pong balls.

May you be buried in a midden of bird bones & soup ladles,
      ignored by archaeologists, forgotten by all.

May you always be the lonely poker player,
      detached and confident, doomed to lose.

May you ride your lurching sled over the fan-tails
      of *sastrugi* snowdrifts, no home in sight,
      no point to give you bearings.

May life remain as puzzling today
      as when you first discovered it.

No. Let everything be explained to you,
      leaving nothing to imagination or learning.

May you take small comfort in your memories.

Let your only company be a team of depressed angels
      trapped in the past.

O that your mouths be plugged with wads of grass
    as you lie for centuries beneath the surface
    in a bed of schist.

Go! Head to sea in an offshore wind.

Spend years adrift among the frozen cracks.

We are bored with all your ballyhoo & noise!

You are the reason we turned off.

Three Poems after OuLiPo

1. In This House, on This Morning
            (a poem written as a 'chimera')

A plane will glide more easily if rubbed with a candle—
remember to relight the pilot. Light bulbs
last longer and give off more light if you strain them
through old stockings. Use nylons to store opinions.
During a power cut the same rules apply: electricity & water
make a recipe—use it as a jigsaw puzzle.

An electric light bulb makes a good mushroom.
Bread can be used to remove light stains.
Dab luminous paint on light switches. Remember
if the head is allowed to dry out completely
when not in use it will crack and break up—
take it off and unplug the holes with a darning needle.

When hanging a long day, nap in the right direction.
Run a bar of soap along the wrong side and monitor its progress
as you pull it through. Try not to interrupt your work
if you're painting ceilings, walls or floors
as this will tend to make them perish. Use a whisk
to save time. Save time by keeping near the phone.

As your children grow older they are easier to let down.
Prevent this by putting a ball of cotton wool in the end of each
        finger.
Write letters and seal them with a little egg white.
Always iron the paper and avoid going in a straight line.
Stagger the line while greasing spots on separate sheets.
Wipe the line clean and free of water droplets.

Put a piece of white paper under each foot. Smooth
some French chalk or talcum over the area before you start
then rub a little paraffin inside your shoes to smarten up
a limp lettuce. If all else fails, scour a blocked drain
in this manner: make an X incision in the stem
and check for cracks in folding leaves. Float in the cistern.

Fold in air bubbles for a fluffier poem. Restore a dented
ping pong ball. To make an inconspicuous join
sew decorative patches over worn out places & feelings—
it is easier with an odd number than an even.
International symbols in pattern books make excellent
wastepaper baskets; chilli sauce an unusual cat repellent.

Use manners as a small vice. Slip your hands into plastic
sandwich bags. If you can't change the water every day
use a pastry brush to remove fluff from working parts. If you
        can,
use eyebrow tweezers to pull out stray pieces—you will find it
easier to extract what you want. Put the stone back
into the avocado and seal. And lastly, the skirting.

2. *Quote It's a Man's World Unquote*

(A poem written using 'Word +7')

It's a man's world
it's a manacle world
it's a managers' world
it's a manageable world
it's a mandala world
it's a mandatory world
it's a mannequin world
it's a manicure world
it's a mange world
it's a mangle world
it's a mania world
it's a manual world
it's a manifest world
it's a manifesto world
it's a manifold world
it's a manky world
it's a manipulate world
it's a manna world
it's a mannerist world
it's a manoeuvre world
it's a manslaughter world
it's a mañana world
it's a manuscript world
it's a mantra world
it's a mantrap world
it's a manure world
it's a manner of world

3. *What is Poetry?*

(A homophonic translation)

Thing.

A song.

A sixth sense.

A puppet.

Rather wry.

Foreign.

Trendy.

Black words.

Naked in the mind.

What the poem is.

Open.

The words begin tearing.

Isn't it attentiveness?

Sex before aching.

A Miscellany of Birds

1. An Abecedary

This morning in my garden I identified with my guidebook, an Arctic Tern, a Bunting, and a Chough. Some Dabchicks, Eider and Francolin. A Grackle, a Hobby, an Ibis and Jackdaw. Kittiwakes, Linnets and Mallards. A Nuthatch and Ouzel. Ptarmigan, Quail, a Ruff and a Reeve. A Skua and Teal. *Upupa epopos*, the orange-headed hoopoe. A visitant Vireo. Wigeons. *Xanthocephalus xanthocephalus*, the yellow-headed blackbird. Yellowhammers and a flock of migrant song sparrows, *Zonotrichia melodia*.

Like everyone else who has had this new experience, I feel the grace through my body, sense the change and flex my wings accordingly.

2. *A Mythology of Birds*

May the Gadwall of Foula
unite with the Serin of Saltee
and the Turnstone of Fetlar
befriend the Great Pochard of Noss.

May the Siskin of Slapton heal wounds
with the Whimbrel of Whalsay
and the Scaup of Porthgwara
forgive the Smew of Hoy,

for the Stint of Sula Sgeir is returned
and the Ruff of Rathlin risen from his sleep!
May the Garganey of Blasket sing forevermore
sweet madrigals with Radipole's majestic Twite!

At Sizewell

A sign painter put the phrase up here in jest:
Zero Weather. Now, none but depressives
sun themselves on the shingle; their ration
of bravado squatting like a leathery old man
beside his bored grandsons. The beach itself
can manage no more than a crawl to the surf.
We knit arms under the elephant sky.
Reluctant to remain, you point to the horizon:
"This place is neither dead nor alive," you wheeze.
With the exception of some fast departing geese
no signs can prove you wrong, save out at sea
the phosphorescent streak astern a North Sea ferry
catching the eye and—if you look just hard enough—
a pod of sea-monsters breaking the green of the waves.

Burning Down the House

'Is it not indeed a pleasure when friends visit from afar?'
—from *The Analects of Confucius*

Gert & Flann arrived on thunderous roadbikes
throttling the peace of the mountain air.
They peeled themselves from their leathers
like snakes sloughing skins and came inside.
'Supplies!' they beamed, raising whiskey bottles.
You came round to meet us from the garden

whistling *An English Country Garden.*
'I thought I heard you pull up. Love the bikes!'
Then you saw the brandished whiskey bottles.
'Jesus Christ!' you said, not holding any airs
or graces. 'Just leave your things inside;
you must have boiled in those leathers.'

Once they'd freshened up and shelved their leathers
we set to the business of drinking in the garden.
The fire of the whiskey teased our insides.
We admired—and they extolled—the roadbikes.
'1200's,' they said. 'Fly faster than air!'
I wondered how that felt and passed the bottle.

By midnight we'd emptied both the bottles.
'So, how d'they ride?' I asked. 'Get the leathers!'
Flann yelled. Your look of disbelief cut the air.
Before I knew it we had left the garden
and a fire burned in the engines of the roadbikes.
Lingering, you fetched a coat; left a candle lit inside

the dark cottage. Madly, Gert & Flann drove inside
each other, their unprotected heads fragile as bottles.
When they stopped, breathless, they offered me a bike.
'I can't,' I said. 'You can; give the man some leathers!'
and suddenly I was flying away from the garden,
my face buffeted by the sober mountain air.

When we returned to the cottage, the air
smelled strange, like burning rubber. From inside,
the flicker of growing flames lit the garden.
'Christ, the candle! Fire!' you screamed, your bottled
fears exploding. Flann gave the door a leathering.
Flames leapt into the night like hellbikes.

We stood in the garden—a row of smashed bottles.
Smoke plumed the air. Flann dashed inside and smothered
the flames with his leathers. Behind us, the roadbikes glinted.

Heavenward

(for Paul Clark)

We clung to the fire like ungulates around straw
bales in a muddy field, as friends levitated
friends from a wooden chair. The initiates
awaited lift-off, framed by a fire-lit team of four

who tried to raise them high on outstretched
fingers. When no lift came the real voodoo
began. Piling our hands above the subject's
head, we summoned a seismic power—gurus

round our live mandala—and when the heat convected
between our joined palms, we dug our fingers
underneath the pilot's arms & legs and bingo!
up they flew, light as air, on heavenward vectors.

Paul debunked the feat as apery: 'A hoax,
a fluke; it's simple kinaesthetics!'
His faithlessness soon stirred our scorn. We coaxed
him into trying it; made him sit with his thin

arms folded by the fire, resolved to demonstrate
a man could *not* be raised without our preparations.
But as we grasped beneath his arms and crooked
knees, we snatched him high in one clean swoop

without the prior ritual, lifting him far beyond return
and Paul went on flying, up & up beyond the cusp of reason,
into the dark stratosphere, his distant cries invoking Newton,
as we bayed below for his witch's blood, like peasants at a
        burning.

Devon Apples

(for Marcus Vergette)

Spring break-up on the frozen river,
the orchard silenced except for the buzz
of insects dreaming this year's apple blossom:
'Come autumn we'll make cider, next May get drunk . . .'

~

Longstem's drunk with new ideas,
Blue Sweet knows they trickle down.
Hollow Core turns art into conception,
Loral Drain has purity of form.

Dufflin celebrates the new millennium,
Hoary Morning struggles with the past.
Slack Ma Girdle exploits its possibilities,
Keswick Codling isn't much impressed.

Sour Natural is coolly received by the British,
Jacob's Strawberry can't dispel the myth.
Johnny Voun redefines melody & phrasing,
Johnny Andrew's audience laughs & laughs.

~

All Doer says we're in this together,
Ben's Red was raised in the heart of the machine.
Bowden's Seedling never found a job,
Coleman's Seedling thinks the price too high.

Breadfruit have fallen out of the system,
Broomhouse Whites will fret about their debts.
Chisel Jersey trembles on the brink of revolution,
Catshead lays the consciousness to come.

Buttery d'Or witnessed a terrible beauty,
Bickington Gray saw the same thing in Europe.
Gilliflower uttered a cry of defiance,
Captain Broad sent worried letters home.

Honey Pin belongs to a circle of extremists,
Improved Pound plants stories in the patriotic press.
Quarrenden mourns glories past in empires lost,
Goring never insisted on the facts.

Early Bowers were bloodthirsty butchers,
Ellis's Bitter killed for political belief.
King Byerd admired the ancient Romans,
Golden Ball demanded the King's execution.

~

Barum met Beef when each needed the other,
Beech Bearer keeps a bottle beneath the bed.
Loyal Drong said not to bother looking,
Reynold's Peach found it just below the surface.

Sops In Wine have married and live abroad,
Crimson Victoria had second thoughts about leaving.
Woolbrook feels at home with Saw Pit,
Quoinings are ready to be themselves.

Plumderity devotes their all to Cerif,
Stockbear & Sugar Bush find they are strangers.
Queen Caroline always keeps her vigil,
The Rattler rivals her sister's best.

Plum Vite announces the evening menu,
Polly White Hair doesn't bother to dress.
No Pip pays the conjuror,
Morgan Sweet does a graceful turn.

～

Sweet Alford needs the church,
Sweet Cleave plays cards in cafés.
Pig's Nose huffs predictably,
Pig's Snout fits the mouth.

Sweet Copin enjoys a different perspective,
Tan Harvey comes into her own.
Tale Sweet announces her pregnancy,
Summer Stubbard's wish was granted.

Thin Skin exerts a mystical pull,
Tom Putt is a person of wisdom & grace.
Nine Square aggravated his heart problem,
Limberlimb was also pale.

Lucombe's Pine let small things slip,
Hangy Down tightened up on them later.
John Toucher was ready for anything,
Long Bit & Listener achieved nothing at all.

Tommy Knight clung to outdated ideas,
Tommy Potter always had the acumen.
Rawlings made final arrangements in silence,
Winter Peach died young—forgive her all.

Billy White lies in theatre for hours,
Butterbox touches a sensitive nerve.
Oaken Pin kisses your lips,
Sidney Strake takes their final breath.*

---

*The names of the apples are all genuine varieties of Devon apple, or varieties which have a close association with the county.

Audubon Becomes Obsessed with Birds

because, as a prelude to mating, the male brings home a gift of food and sings;

because both birds & whales sing;

because both birds & whales migrate—*ergo* birds are the souls of whales;

because you need a compass and a map to migrate accurately;

because migrating birds have both;

because the ancient mariners learned to navigate from birds;

because steamer ducks, penguins, ratites and emus, ostriches, rheas, cassowaries and kiwis, Galapagos cormorants and a grebe from the Andean lakes are all truly grounded;

because the New Zealand Takahe, the Mesites, the Rails and the Kagu cannot take off either;

because the Dodo, the Mascarene Solitaire, the Great Auk and the Elephant-bird might still exist today, if only they had flown;

because the Romans tagged their legs with coloured rags to tell the folks at home the name of He who won the chariot race;

because Greek sages practised divination from the flight of birds;

because the Rongorongo tablets of Easter Island tell of *The Rite of The Sacred Birdman*;

because the scribes of ancient Egypt saw Existence rise from Non-Existence in the shape of the *Bennu Bird*;

because the *Bennu Bird* becomes the *Phoenix* of the Greeks;

because the *Phoenix* builds a nest of scented branches, starts a fire and is consumed by flames;

because the Romans saw *Aquarius* as a heaven-flying bird;

because the Maya saw *Aquarius* as *Coz*, the *Celestial Falcon*;

because the ancient Hindus called *Aquarius 'Garuda'*, the Birdman; vehicle of Vishnu, the *Preserver*;

because these myths mix birds, astronomy and water into symbols of rebirth and life;

because birds know what time it is;

because vultures gathering indicate dead men;

because birds are like ideas—they visit us fleetingly, then disappear.

Fall of the Rebel Angels

Life used to be a string of lazy Sundays,
but the heyday doesn't last long, does it?
We sit drink wine and talk to fill the void
now the subtle differences between
solitude & loneliness have vanished.
We have become as strangers to ourselves,
wearing our opinions & beliefs;
grand theories slung across the shoulders
like wings. But they can be frail, as if hung
with a peg on a line—a tissue covering—
to distract us from the task of listening.
Life is so tentative a proposition, it bears
away the little that we know, like winds
tearing off a clutch of leaves; a blossom.

Printed in the United Kingdom
by Lightning Source UK Ltd.
116355UKS00001B/163-180

9 781844 712809